Sights and Scenes at the Lewis and Clark Centennial Exposition Portland, Oregon.

Very Completely Illustrating the Fair

PRICE 25c

PUBLISHED BY ROBERT A. REID, PORTLAND, OREGON

Mailed by Publisher on receipt of price. Address Robert A. Reid, 289 Alder Street, Portland, Ore.

Copyright, 1905, by Robert A. Reid. All Rights Reserved

PRINTED BY BUSHONG & CO.
ENGRAVINGS BY HICKS-CHATTEN ENGRAVING CO.
PHOTOGRAPHS BY STRONG, FORD, COHEN, THE OFFICIAL
PHOTOGRAPHIC CO., AND OTHERS

THE PIONEER

RCB CLASSIC REPRINT
Hidden Light Private Press 2016
Printed in the United States of America
Rose City Books @ www.rosecitybooks.com

ISBN 978-1-365-56232-7   90000

THE PORTLAND FAIR OF 1905

This little book gives a pictorial description of the Exposition of 1905, which commemorates the Centennial of the exploration of the Oregon Territory, by an expedition led by Captains Meriwether Lewis and William Clark, who were the first white men to cross the continent. The success of these explorers resulted in the acquisition of the great Oregon Country by the United States. The Lewis and Clark Exposition is situated amidst most beautiful and picturesque surroundings. While other expositions have had beauties created by the skill and study of landscape artists and designers, nature has here bestowed attractions unapproachable by the hand of man. The forest-clad hillsides, the distant snow-capped mountain peaks, and the lake and river waters lend to the vision a scene of entrancing beauty and grandeur. Among these scenes have been built the great structures which house the products of the labors of man. Here hours and days may be profitably spent in gaining knowledge and enjoyment. The Exhibit Palaces and the Government Building offer an endless variety of interesting subjects; some of the State Buildings contain complete expositions of their respective states. Then there is The Trail, the aggregation of amusement enterprises provided for the pleasure of the people. Centennial Park, with its cool, shady hillsides always invites the weary sightseer to pleasant rest. At night, with approaching darkness, the great buildings become brilliant with thousands of electric lights, while the walks and grounds are illuminated with fairyland splendor.

The field, the forest and the fisheries; the mine and the manufactures, mercantile pursuits and the school, all these principal factors in the active life of the people are here represented, showing the vast progress of the Pacific Northwest, stamping the Lewis and Clark Exposition as a successful enterprise and a fitting expression of the gratitude of a patriotic people.

FORESTRY BUILDING

Most unique and one of the most attractive structures on the grounds. It is 100 feet wide and 200 feet long.
It is emblematic of one of the greatest sources of wealth of Oregon.

ORIENTAL EXHIBITS PALACE

This Palace contains wares from Japan, East India, Egypt, Turkey and Persia. The galleries contain the notable Oregon Educational Exhibit. It is 150 feet wide and 260 long.

EUROPEAN EXHIBITS BUILDING

Here in a structure 100 by 450 feet are displayed products from Hungary, Italy, Austria, Holland, Switzerland, Germany and the British Possessions.

LOOKING TOWARD EXHIBIT PALACES FROM THE TRAIL.

This picture shows a portion of Centennial Park, with some of the State Buildings and Exhibit Palaces beyond.

THE AGRICULTURAL PALACE

The structure is 200 by 450 feet, and contains exhibits from twenty-four Oregon Counties, and from five other Northwestern States.

HITTING THE TRAIL

This stirring scene represents the Cowboys of a former day out for sport and engaged in "Shooting up the town."

PALACE OF MANUFACTURES, LIBERAL ARTS AND VARIED INDUSTRIES

Contains the varied products of many of the foremost manufacturers of our Country. Portland is well
represented. This building is 240 by 430 feet on its long side, and 320 short side.

STATUE OF CAPTAIN MERIWETHER LEWIS
Born in Virginia, 1774.

STATUE OF CAPTAIN WILLIAM CLARK
Born in Virginia, 1770.

BAND STAND AND GRAND STAIRWAY

The Grand Stairway is the principal avenue of travel from the Exhibit Palaces to the Lake Front and Band Stand where music is daily discoursed for the pleasure of the multitude.

MACHINERY, ELECTRICITY AND TRANSPORTATION PALACE

Interesting exhibits are here found in all of these lines, and the Northwestern manufacturers are not without notable representation. The building is 100 by 500 feet with wings on either end 100 by 100 feet each.

EXHIBIT PALACES FROM THE ESPLANADE

One of the beautiful scenes of the Exposition Grounds showing the shelving terraces and winding walks.

THE MINES AND METALLURGY BUILDING

The Mines building, with its peculiarly interesting exhibits, faces the Auditorium across Concourse Plaza. It is 100 feet wide by 200 feet long.

TOTEM POLES

These rude records of the early Alaskans stand near the Alaskan and Philippine wing of the Government Building.

THE GOVERNMENT BUILDING

This magnificent and dignified structure in Spanish Renaissance is 1025 feet in length.   In it is prepared many
an interesting lesson for the people.

THE BRIDGE OF NATIONS

The Bridge of Nations leads from the Trail and Esplanade, connecting them with the Peninsular upon which the Government Buildings are all situated. It spans Guilds Lake and is a striking feature of the scene, both in the sunlight of day and when illuminated at night.

UNITED STATES ALASKAN AND PHILIPPINE EXHIBIT BUILDING
This is the East Wing of the Government Building. The West Wing is devoted to the exhibits of the United States Fish Commission.

UNITED STATES IRRIGATION AND FORESTRY EXHIBIT BUILDING

At the rear of the East Colonnade of the Government Building are housed the exhibits representing these subjects now occupying the attention of our Government, and many eminent men of the day.

UNITED STATES LIFE SAVING STATION

One of the most interesting works done by our Government is that of saving life at the dangerous points upon the Coast. The daily exhibits here given show how hundreds of lives are saved annually.

LOOKING TOWARD FORESTRY BUILDING FROM OREGON AVENUE

The grouping of the various Exhibit Palaces and State Buildings, with the trees surrounding many of them, upon the grounds of the Exposition, causes many attractive avenue scenes and beautiful vistas.

MUSEUM OF ART

The Museum of Fine Arts is just beyond and opposite the Forestry Building. Safety for the priceless contents has caused to be built a fire-proof structure of modest outward appearance, but exceedingly attractive in its interior arrangement and effect.

THE AUDITORIUM

The Auditorium or Festival Hall is a simple yet dignified building facing the Concourse Plaza, well suited for the large gatherings of people always occurring at Expositions. It has seating capacity for 2500.

THE SUNKEN GARDENS

The Sunken Gardens, simple and beautiful, are an object lesson. Why should not every new American town and city have such in its centre? Here and there are towns which do have such spots so selected.

THE BUFFALO DANCE

One of the groups of Statuary descriptive of different phases of Indian Life adorning the Exposition Grounds. Standing near the New York State Building.

EXPOSITION BUILDINGS AS THEY FACE LEWIS AND CLARK AVENUE
This view shows the relative positions of the Exhibit Palaces. The L-shaped Building at the left is the Art
Museum, opposite is the Forestry Building, to the right of which is the Oriental Palace, then
Foreign Exhibits, Agricultural Palace, and Manufactures, Liberal Arts and Varied
Industries, in their respective order.

ADMINISTRATION BUILDING

This building, devoted to the business transactions of the Exposition, stands at the left after entering,
between the entrance and the more pretentious Colonnade entrance. The offices of
the President and Directors and Chiefs of Departments are all located in the
Administration Building.

COLONNADE ENTRANCE

Just within the outer gates, a pleasant greeting to the eye, is this graceful Colonnade, of
Corinthian Pillars.

VIEW ON LEWIS AND CLARK AVENUE

Lewis and Clark Avenue is the most prominent thoroughfare of the Exposition Grounds, running east and west. All the greater exhibit palaces have end fronts facing it. The statuary, "Hitting the Trail," is one of its other prominent features. The Art Museum is at the extreme west end and Concourse Plaza at the east end.

OREGON STATE BUILDING

Here the Sons and Daughters of the Hostess State may rest and meet in friendly intercourse. The commodious
structure stands at the left just within the Colonnade entrance.

MASSACHUSETTS STATE BUILDING

The Old Bay State, mother of American pioneers, stretched her hand across the continent and set up this beautiful building.

INTERIOR VIEW IN MASSACHUSETTS' BUILDING

The building is overflowing with exhibits of Education and kindred Arts and Sciences, and historical scenes and events are pictured on all sides.

WASHINGTON STATE BUILDING

Palatial edifice occupying a crowning site, worthy of the growing and prosperous cities and
towns of the great Northwestern State.

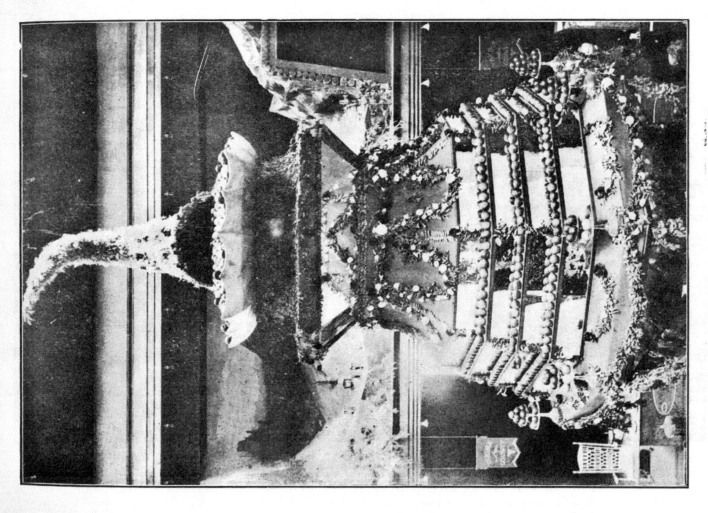

INTERIOR WASHINGTON STATE BUILDING

This building has many bays and rooms lavishly displaying various principal industries of the State. The "Horn of Plenty," shown above, is typical of her abundant crops,

CALIFORNIA STATE BUILDING

Nothing could be more neighborly and show finer sentiment than the manner in which the people of the great
State with Golden Gate have come to the Exposition and erected this immense palatial structure,
emblematic of her early architecture, and filled with her products of today.

INTERIOR OF CALIFORNIA STATE BUILDING

A rich profusion of all semi-tropical fruits are here displayed, and in many a fanciful form. A bear made of prunes, the State Capitol from English walnuts, an elephant also of nuts.

THE BAND STAND AND PALACE OF AGRICULTURE AT NIGHT.

The illuminations at the Exposition at night are worth traveling far to see. Seen from the Bridge of Nations, this view is simply a part of a glorious picture. The outlines are duplicated in the mirror of the lake, where they sway and palpitate as the water is agitated or rippled by the gondoliers' oars. The Exposition should be seen by day and by night.

COWBOY AT REST

Contemplation of the transitory life on the plains and a prophetic vision must frequently have possessed the minds of these active men, first invaders of the prairies.

NEW YORK STATE BUILDING

This is one of the gems of architecture, beautifully situated at the right of the main picture, looking from Lake View Terrace, beyond the Sunken Gardens.

THE MISSOURI STATE BUILDING

The late Exposition State has placed this building here not only as a reciprocal courtesy, but to welcome to it her thousands of former sons and daughters.

THE ILLINOIS STATE BUILDING
A representation of the Springfield home of Abraham Lincoln. Nothing could show plainer than does this many-windowed, two-story building, that the strength of the nation lies in the middle class, who live in modest homes, for from them comes the guiding power in times of tranquil national life and the heroes in time of struggle.

IDAHO STATE BUILDING

A substantial, roomy, handsome structure, inviting to rest and to an inspection of the attractions offered by this great State.

UTAH STATE BUILDING

Crowning the eminence rising from Guild Lake and beyond the Idaho Building stands the graceful Utah Building, showing the enterprise of her people and the products of the State.

COLORADO STATE BUILDING

This structure is entirely devoted to the display of specimens of the State's agricultural products, which comprises 65 per cent. of her annual wealth production.

AGRICULTURAL EXPERIMENTAL GARDENS.
These Experimental Gardens are over beyond Centennial Park. Of the most vital interest to farmers
are the subjects demonstrated. Beyond the Experimental Grounds is the camp
of the Exposition Guards.

THE MAINE STATE BUILDING.

A reproduction of the birthplace of America's greatest poet, Longfellow, who was born at Portland, Maine, February 27, 1807.

THE UNITED STATES BUILDING AT NIGHT

Little less at night than in the daylight is the Government Building a principal attraction, with its lines illuminated against the sky.

THE YOUNG WOMEN'S CHRISTIAN ASSOCIATION BUILDING

This hospitable resting place is conveniently located at the rear end of the Palace of Manufactures, Liberal Arts and Varied Industries.   It has a well conducted restaurant.

THE AMERICAN INN

This vast Exposition Hotel, the only hotel within the grounds, measuring 346x458 feet, with its 600 rooms, constructed so substantially, and the entire American Inn business is the direct result of the enterprise of an American woman.

VIEW FROM IDAHO TERRACE

One of the charming views of the Exposition's "Main Picture" is to be had from Idaho's State Building looking across to the Grand Stairway, Centennial Park and the forest-clad hills beyond.

A STEP TOWARDS CIVILIZATION

Group of statuary in Concourse Plaza, of Indian life, showing the beginning of the adoption of the white man's ways.

SOME EXHIBITS WITHIN THE FORESTRY BUILDING

The contents of Forestry Building are in keeping with the exterior. The specimens of extraordinary wide planks are most remarkable, while Oregon's fish culture and forest animals are well represented. In the galleries are about 300 of the wonderful Curtis Indian Prints, a fine exposition of Indian life in themselves.

NATIONAL CASH REGISTER COMPANY'S LECTURE PAVILION

The Welfare Work lectures given in this building by representatives of the National Cash Register Co., of Dayton, Ohio, demonstrate the practicability of applying the golden rule to the business relations of employe and employer. The methods adopted by the company with its five thousand people is worthy the study of all employers and all of our people.

THE MASONIC BUILDING

Headquarters for Masons, and Order of Eastern Star, an organization of ladies who are mothers, wives, sisters or daughters of Masons. It is opposite the Forestry Building.

THE EXPOSITION HOSPITAL

A model hospital set up to meet all emergencies which may occur when great concourses of people assemble.
It is prettily located near Centennial Park, a quiet locality within the grounds.

THE HUMAN FLAG

This was one of the patriotic demonstrations, composed of children dressed in red, white and blue and stars, occurring upon Athletic Field at the Exposition, under the management of Multnomah Chapter, Daughters of the American Revolution.

MILKING TIME

Milking time is modeled out of pure butter. It is a favorite subject and attracts the attention of all visitors. It is in the Washington State Building.

WASCO COUNTY EXHIBIT

This is one of the typical county exhibits in Agricultural Palace, where they vie in friendly rivalry for the first prize for their products.

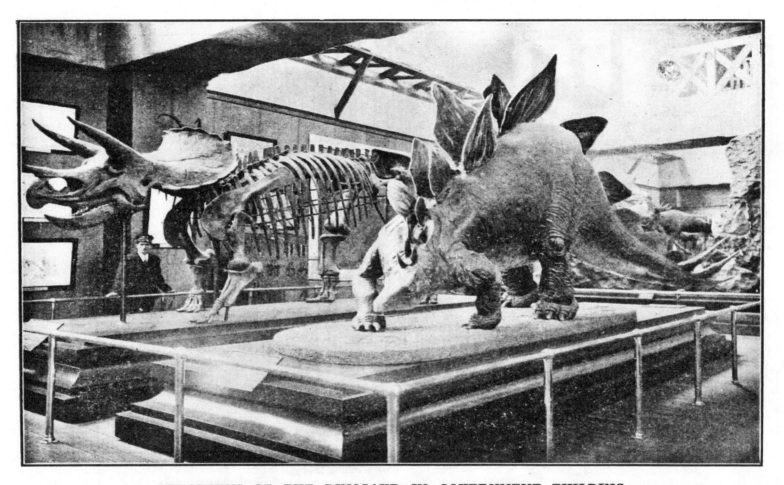

SPECIMENS OF THE DINOSAUR IN GOVERNMENT BUILDING

These mammoth specimens of reptiles were restored by aid of parts of the skeletons found in Wyoming. They represent a class of animal life existing on our continent in prehistoric times.

MONUMENT TO AGRICULTURE

In the central circle in the Palace of Agriculture. "When tillage begins other arts follow. The farmers therefore are the founders of human civilization."—Daniel Webster.

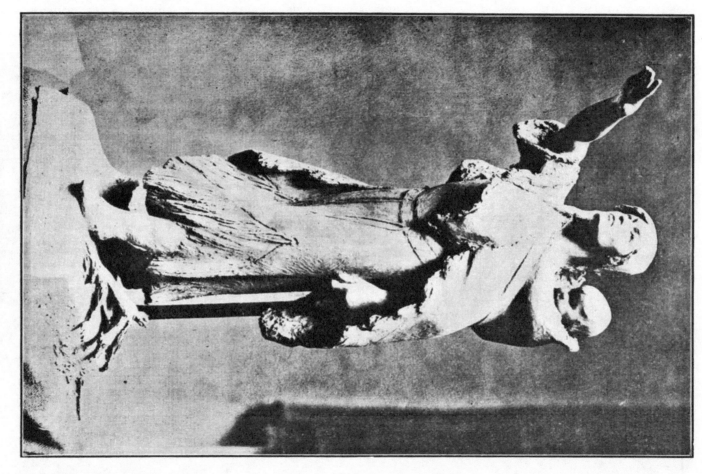

STATUE OF SACAJAWEA

Statue (by Miss Cooper) of the Indian Woman Sacajawea (Birdwoman) who guided Lewis and Clark to the shores of the Pacific. It was cast by Bonnard, in copper, from Oregon mines, given for the purpose. The funds for completion of the monument were raised through the efforts of the members of the patriotic Woman's Club of Portland.

BURNS' COTTAGE

This is a faithful representation of the humble abode of the immortal Scottish poet. It is worthy of time and trouble to visit, as showing the home of one whose fame will never die.

LOOKING TOWARD THE TRAIL

This view taken from Centennial Park shows something of the Trail, the Bridge of Nations, and the palatial Government Building in the distance.

SCENE ON THE TRAIL

The Trail is a new name for the amusement section of an Exposition, especially appropriate for one held in the West.   The Trail has many very attractive features.

FAIR JAPAN

Fair Japan is always attractive and entertaining, with its tea drinking booths, its Geisha girls and Japanese theater. The bazaar also attracts the purchasers of souvenirs.

SCENE IN FAIR JAPAN

Group of Geisha Girls in Fair Japan, on the Trail. The interior of Fair Japan is exceedingly attractive with its nooks and corners in Japanese scenic effects, its Japanese theater and tea and rice cake pavilions. The Japanese girls flutter about like creatures from out a fairy book.

GRAND ENTRANCE TO STREETS OF CAIRO AND BEAUTIFUL ORIENT

One of the principal amusement places on the Trail. A portion of the Orient brought for the pleasure of the people, gay and interesting with its brightly costumed natives and dancers.

PRINCESS RAJAH

The beautiful and famous Oriental dancer in Streets of Cairo and Beautiful Orient, on the Trail.

CORENA   **FATIMA**

Graceful and Supple Oriental Dancers in the Streets of Cairo and Beautiful Orient, on the Trail.

FAIR CAMEL RIDERS

One of the most fascinating and exhilarating pastimes for ladies is riding the camels, afternoons and
evenings in the Streets of Cairo, on the Trail.

THE LAND OF THE MID-NIGHT SUN

This is an electrical scenic production which portrays with wonderful fidelity of detail a remarkable trip of thousands of miles over land and sea and fields of snow and ice from Portland to Dawson City, the Frozen North, and Land of the Mid-Night Sun. The scenes are wonderfully beautiful.

SHOOTING THE CHUTES

This is fine sport for both participants and onlookers, and the Chutes, as here erected, is one of the finest
built. It is patronized by old and young.

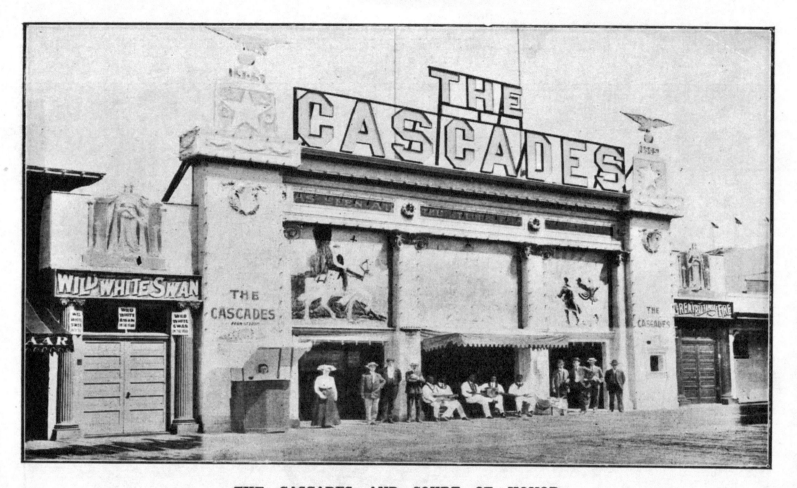

THE CASCADES AND COURT OF HONOR

The central and crowning glory of the great World's Fair at St. Louis was the Cascades with the great
circular Festival Hall and the Colonnade of States in the background, all producing the
most magnificent architectural display ever seen. All is here reproduced
with electrical and water scenes most faithfully pictured.

TEMPLE OF MIRTH

There is a time for everything. The time to laugh is soon after entering the Temple of Mirth, at least every one does laugh after entering. The contortion mirrors placed about the halls cause every one to be glad that one really looks as one does, rather than as one might.

THE HAUNTED CASTLE.

The Haunted Castle is filled with a variety of illusions, optical and physical, which keep the audience looking, wondering and laughing.

THE INFANT INCUBATORS

The way in which science and scientific nursing steps in and assists in preserving infantile life is here shown in a most interesting and instructive manner.

A TRIP TO SIBERIA

Russia, always a land of mysterious interest, is now even more than ever interesting. This trip enables the visitors to learn very much about Russian life and scenery.

JABOUR'S WILD ANIMAL ARENA

This is the Trained Animal Concession on the Trail, and the performances show to what a high state of intelligence animals may be brought by patient teaching.

THE HOME OF TRIXIE, THE EDUCATED HORSE

Trixie is a wonderfully well educated horse. His ability to understand the human voice and to reason things out is marvellous. The plunge of the trained high diving elks as here exhibited is very startling.

KLONDIKE GOLD MINING EXHIBIT
Within the extensive building, in most realistic way, there is presented a practical and actual illustration of the method of placer mining as pursued in the Klondike gold regions. The subject of gold mining is one which never loses interest to the human family.

THE GRAND SNOW-CAPPED MT. HOOD, SEEN ACROSS THE EXPOSITION CITY

Not every day may Mt. Hood be seen at its best, for clouds ever hover 'round it, but the constant watcher
is frequently rewarded by seeing it stand forth clearly and glisten in the sunlight
as a mountain of silver. It is 11,225 feet high.

MULTNOMAH FALLS

Falling 840 feet the Multnomah Falls are the highest, most beautiful and most renowned of the Columbian Falls. It is 32 miles distant from Portland, up the Columbia.

CRATER LAKE.

Crater Lake, although comparatively little known to the American public, is one of the greatest natural scenic wonders of the world. It is situated in the Cascade Range in Southern Oregon, 8000 feet above the sea level, and is the highest body of water existing. Its bed is the crater of an extinct volcano, circular in shape, the lake being about five miles in diameter. It exceeds 2000 feet in depth, is fed by the melting snows and rainfall and has no visible outlet. The cliff sides forming the rim vary from 500 to 2000 feet in height. Its waters are a bright azure blue varying with other brilliant shadings caused by the purity of the water, great depth and bright colored bottom. It is classed with Niagara Falls, the Yosemite Valley, the Grand Canyons of Colorado and the Yellowstone in its impressiveness. It recently became, by act of congress, one of the National Parks, and will, undoubtedly soon be opened by rail to the public. "The beauty and majesty of the scenery are indescribable."

TACOMA, AND MOUNT TACOMA
From which the city got its name.

CHARTERED FOR WHEAT

The total shipment out of Portland in 1904 of Wheat and Flour was 12,000,000 bushels.

SCENE IN PORTLAND HARBOR

Although already one of the leading waterways of trade, Portland Harbor is yet in its infancy
as a center of export and ocean traffic.

A MONARCH OF THE FOREST

This great tree, 8 feet in diameter, is not an uncommon specimen. "The Woods are full of them." In 1904 Oregon's lumber output was valued at $12,650,000.

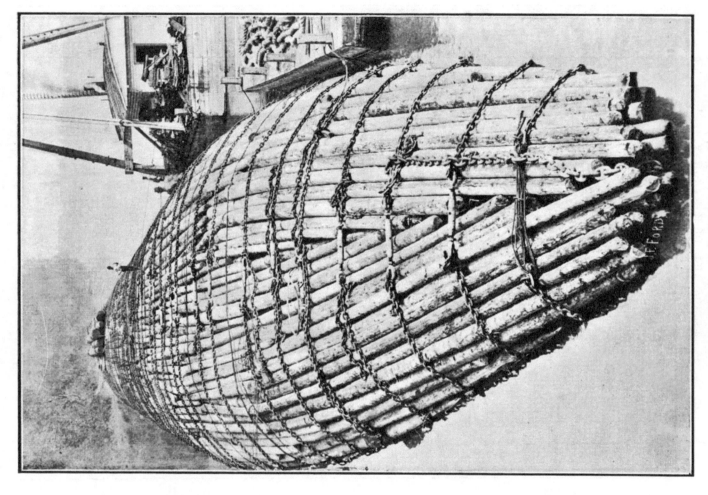

GREAT SEA-GOING LOG RAFT

One of many towed to San Francisco; 56 by 720 feet and 24 feet deep; contained 8,000,000 feet lumber measure. Value about $30,000.

DRAWING IN THE NETS WITH THE SALMON CATCH

The total value of the Oregon Fisheries for the year 1904 was $3,500,000.

SALMON READY FOR THE OPERATION OF CANNING
The largest Salmon Canneries in the World are located along the Columbia River.

A PASTORAL SCENE—GREAT FLOCK OF OREGON SHEEP

Picture of 1500 Sheep taken as they were about starting out to graze for the day. Oregon's wool clip for 1904 was valued at three millions of dollars.

OREGON INDIANS

Members of the Wishem Tribe of Indians, who were once a large and powerful race, commanding the Columbia River Territory. They were, by turns, both friends and foes of the White Man.

THE PORTLAND

The Portland is the finest hotel in Portland and easily ranks as first-class among the hotels of the country. It is centrally located in the heart of the City, yet with quiet surroundings. It is a center for social events, for the meeting of prominent people, and as a high-toned place for long and short sojourns for travelers and tourists.

WASHINGTON STREET, LOOKING WEST

Washington Street is the division street of the City. There are other prominent and busy streets, but Washington is the principal business thoroughfare. Upon it real estate prices soar the highest.

COMING OF THE WHITE MAN

Fine Work of Art in Portland City Park, depicting conflicting emotions in the countenance of the Red Man, caused by the coming of the White Man.

15169097R00058